baked & delicious

a visual step-by-step guide to perfect baking

This edition published in 2012
LOVE FOOD is an imprint of Parragon Books Ltd

Parragon
Queen Street House
4 Queen Street
Bath BA1 1HE, UK

ISBN: 978-1-4454-7861-6

Printed in China

Additional photography by Mike Cooper
Introduction by Linda Doeser
New recipes by Christine Last
Photography by Mike Cooper
Home economy by Lincoln Jefferson

Notes for the Reader
This book uses both metric and imperial measurements. Follow the same units of measurement
throughout; do not mix metric and imperial. All spoon measurements are level: teaspoons are
assumed to be 5 ml, and tablespoons are assumed to be 15 ml. Unless otherwise stated, milk is
assumed to be full fat, eggs and individual vegetables are medium, and pepper is freshly ground
black pepper.

The times given are an approximate guide only. Preparation times differ according to the techniques
used by different people and the cooking times may also vary from those given. Optional ingredients,
variations or serving suggestions have not been included in the calculations.

Recipes using raw or very lightly cooked eggs should be avoided by infants, the elderly, pregnant
women, convalescents and anyone suffering from an illness. Pregnant and breastfeeding women are
advised to avoid eating peanuts and peanut products. Sufferers from nut allergies should be aware
that some of the ready-made ingredients used in the recipes in this book may contain nuts. Always
check the packaging before use.

contents

introduction

This magnificent cookbook, with its profusion of beautiful and immensely useful photographs, will prove to be an invaluable addition to any cook's bookshelf. The recipes are clear, easy to follow, beautifully illustrated and simply scrumptious, so whatever your level of expertise in the kitchen you are virtually guaranteed success every time.

Every recipe starts with a photograph of all the ingredients, but this is more than just a pretty picture or – even less helpful – a montage that is not to scale so that a pear appears to be the same size as an egg. Instead, it serves as a handy way of checking that you have everything ready before you start cooking. Just comparing the picture with the ingredients arranged on your own worktop or kitchen table will ensure that you haven't missed anything out and when it's time to add the glacé cherries, for example, you have already quartered them as specified in the ingredients list. If you're uncertain about how thinly to slice fruit or how dark to toast nuts, a glance at the photograph will provide an instant answer.

Each short and straightforward step of the method is clearly explained without any jargon or difficult technical terms. Once again, what you see in the photograph is what you should expect to see in front of you. Not only is this reassuring for the novice cook, those with more experience will find it a helpful reminder of the little touches that can easily be overlooked. Each recipe also has a mouth-watering photograph of the finished cake, biscuits, tart or loaf.

why you need this book

Even some quite experienced cooks find 'baking' a daunting prospect and think it's sure to be difficult. Yet the word baking encompasses many different kinds of products from biscuits to bread and a variety of different techniques from creamed sponge cakes to choux pastry. They can't all be impossibly difficult and demanding and, in fact, most are astonishingly easy. In this book there are 60 easy-to-follow recipes for cakes, traybakes, sweet and savoury pastries, biscuits and bread – some traditional family favourites and others with a contemporary twist, some for special occasions and others for everyday treats. All of them are straightforward and, by using the unique frame-by-frame guide, even the novice cook will find they're figuratively and literally a piece of cake.

top tips for easy baking

- Read all the way through the recipe – ingredients list and method – before you start, so that you know exactly what you will need. Scrabbling about at the back of the cupboard to find an ingredient or moving half a dozen other utensils to reach the one you need in the middle of baking is, at best, exasperating and, at worst, liable to spoil it.

- Follow the recipe instructions for cooling. Some cakes and biscuits are fragile and should be left to firm up before turning out onto a wire cooling rack. Others should be turned out immediately, or the base will become soggy. Heavy cakes are usually allowed to cool completely in the tin.

- When making pastry dough, collect the dry ingredients together ready for use and put a jug of water in the refrigerator to chill – keeping the dough cold is essential for crisp results.

- Accurate measurement of the ingredients is more important for baking than for any other kind of cooking. Weigh dry ingredients on reliable kitchen scales and measure liquids in a measuring jug or, for small quantities, standard measuring spoons.

- Bread recipes often require yeast and may specify using hand-hot liquid. Yeast works best at a temperature of 21–36°C/70–97°F. Do not use hotter water as this will kill the yeast and prevent it from producing the gases that cause the bread to rise.

- Always preheat the oven to the specified temperature. An oven that is not hot enough will cause baked goods to sink, while one that is too hot can cause them to crack. If you're unsure about the reliability of your thermostat, invest in an oven thermometer and use that to check the temperature.

- The type of flour used for baking is important, and substituting one for another may produce disappointing results. Plain flour is predominantly used for pastry dough and anything that does not need a raising agent, whereas self-raising flour has added baking powder and is used for lighter bakes, such as cakes. Strong bread flour has a high gluten content that produces an elastic dough when kneaded and wholemeal flour is made from the whole grain and produces a denser, nuttier, slightly more chewy texture than white flour.

- Whatever flour you are using, it is always important to sift it before you begin baking, to add air and remove any lumps, even if it is described as ready-sifted on the packet. You should also sift icing sugar when it is used as an ingredient, or required for dusting.

- Except when you are making pastry dough by the rubbing-in method, collect all your ingredients together, including anything that is normally stored in the refrigerator, at least half an hour before you start cooking, to bring them to room temperature. Eggs are particularly important because if they are too cold when they are added, they tend to curdle. Remove mixing bowls from the cupboard and bring them to room temperature.

time-saving shortcuts

• Melt chocolate in the microwave oven. Break it into pieces and put it into a microwave-proof bowl. Heat on MEDIUM for 10 seconds, then stir. Return to the oven and heat for another 10 seconds before checking and stirring again – even when it's melted it will hold its shape so you cannot tell if it's ready just by looking at it. White chocolate should be heated on LOW.

• The easiest way to peel fruits such as nectarines and peaches, as well as tomatoes, is to slit their skins, put them into a heatproof bowl and pour in boiling water to cover. Leave to stand for 30–60 seconds and drain. The skins will slip off much more easily.

• If dough is sticky, even after chilling in the refrigerator, roll it out between sheets of baking parchment or clingfilm. You can use the bottom sheet to help you transfer it to the baking sheet.

• Toast nuts in the microwave to avoid burning. Spread out 4 tablespoons of nuts on a microwave-proof plate and cook on HIGH for 5 minutes, then leave to cool before preparing.

• When measuring small quantities of something sticky such as honey or syrup, stand the spoon in hot water for a minute. It will then drop off the spoon easily.

• All is not lost if you have forgotten to remove the butter from the refrigerator in advance – just microwave on HIGH for 15–20 seconds.

• Freeze prepared pastry dough to use at a later date. Wrap the dough securely in clingfilm and it will last for up to six months in the freezer. When it's needed, simply defrost, roll out and use as instructed in the recipe, for a quick home-baked treat.

cakes & traybakes

chocolate fudge cake 11
victoria sponge cake 13
classic cherry cake 15
rich almond cake 17
double chocolate mint sponge 19
honey & almond cake 21
orange madeira ring 23
caramel peach gâteau 25
coffee & walnut roulade 27
apple streusel bars 29
frosted carrot cake 31
cinnamon squares 33
chocolate chip brownies 35

chocolate fudge cake

serves 8

ingredients

175 g/6 oz unsalted butter,
  softened, plus extra for greasing
175 g/6 oz golden caster sugar
3 eggs, beaten
3 tbsp golden syrup
40 g/1½ oz ground almonds

175 g/6 oz self-raising flour
pinch of salt
40 g/1½ oz cocoa powder

icing

225 g/8 oz plain chocolate, broken
  into pieces
55 g/2 oz dark muscovado sugar
225 g/8 oz unsalted butter, diced
5 tbsp evaporated milk
½ tsp vanilla extract

11

>1 Preheat the oven to 180°C/350°F/ Gas Mark 4. Grease and line two 20-cm/8-inch sandwich tins.

>2 For the icing, place the ingredients in a saucepan. Heat gently, stirring constantly, until melted. Pour into a bowl and leave to cool. Cover and chill for 1 hour, or until spreadable.

>3 For the cake, place the butter and sugar in a bowl and beat together until light and fluffy. Gradually beat in the eggs. Stir in the golden syrup and almonds.

>4 Sift the flour, salt and cocoa powder into a separate bowl, then fold into the butter mixture. Add a little water, if necessary, to make a dropping consistency.

>5 Spoon the mixture into the prepared tins and smooth the surfaces. Bake in the preheated oven for 30–35 minutes, or until well risen and firm. Transfer to a wire rack to cool.

>6 Sandwich the cakes together with half of the icing. Spread the remaining icing over the top and side of the cake. Serve.

victoria sponge cake

serves 8

ingredients

175 g/6 oz self-raising flour
1 tsp baking powder
175 g/6 oz butter, softened,
   plus extra for greasing

175 g/6 oz golden caster sugar
3 eggs
icing sugar, for dusting

filling

3 tbsp raspberry jam
300 ml/10 fl oz double cream,
   whipped
16 fresh strawberries, halved

> 1
Preheat the oven to 180°C/350°F/
Gas Mark 4. Grease and base-line two
20-cm/8-inch sandwich tins.

> 2
Sift the flour and baking powder into
a bowl. Gradually beat in the butter,
sugar and eggs. Spoon the mixture
into the prepared tins and smooth
the surfaces.

> 3
Bake in the preheated oven for
25–30 minutes, or until well risen and
firm. Transfer to a wire rack to cool.

> 4
Sandwich the cakes together with the
jam, cream and strawberry halves.
Dust with icing sugar and serve.

14

classic cherry cake

serves 8

ingredients

250 g/9 oz glacé cherries,
  quartered
85 g/3 oz ground almonds
200 g/7 oz plain flour

1 tsp baking powder
200 g/7 oz unsalted butter,
  plus extra for greasing
200 g/7 oz caster sugar

3 large eggs
finely grated rind and juice
  of 1 lemon
6 sugar cubes, crushed

> **1** Preheat the oven to 180°C/350°F/ Gas Mark 4. Grease and line a 20-cm/8-inch cake tin.

> **2** Place the cherries, almonds and 1 tablespoon of the flour in a bowl. Sift the remaining flour and baking powder into a separate bowl.

> **3** Place the butter and sugar in a bowl and beat together until light and fluffy. Gradually beat in the eggs.

> **4** Fold the butter mixture, cherry mixture, lemon rind and juice into the flour mixture.

> **5** Spoon the mixture into the prepared tin and smooth the surface. Sprinkle with the crushed sugar cubes. Bake in the preheated oven for 1–1¼ hours, or until well risen and firm.

> **6** Transfer to a wire rack to cool. Serve.

rich almond cake

serves 8

ingredients

butter, for greasing
250 g/9 oz ricotta cheese
4 eggs, separated
1 tsp almond essence
175 g/6 oz golden caster sugar

250 g/9 oz ground almonds
finely grated rind of 1 lime
flaked almonds, to decorate
icing sugar, for dusting

> 1 Preheat the oven to 150°C/300°F/ Gas Mark 2. Grease and line a 23-cm/9-inch cake tin.

> 2 Place the ricotta, egg yolks, almond essence and sugar in a bowl and beat together. Stir in the almonds and lime rind.

> 3 Whisk the egg whites in a separate bowl, until stiff but not dry.

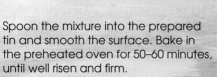

> 4 Fold the egg whites into the ricotta mixture, until evenly combined.

> 5 Spoon the mixture into the prepared tin and smooth the surface. Bake in the preheated oven for 50–60 minutes, until well risen and firm.

> 6 Transfer to a wire rack to cool. Sprinkle with flaked almonds, dust with icing sugar and serve.

double chocolate mint sponge

serves 8

ingredients

150 g/5½ oz plain flour

2 tbsp cocoa powder

1 tbsp baking powder

175 g/6 oz unsalted butter, softened, plus extra for greasing

175 g/6 oz caster sugar

3 eggs, beaten

1 tbsp milk

40 g/1½ oz chocolate mint sticks, chopped

140 g/5 oz chocolate spread, plus extra to drizzle

chocolate mint sticks to decorate

> 1

Preheat the oven to 180°C/350°F/ Gas Mark 4. Grease and line two 20-cm/8-inch sandwich tins.

> 2

Sift the flour, cocoa and baking powder into a bowl. Gradually beat in the butter, sugar and eggs. Stir in the milk and chocolate mint pieces.

> 3

Spoon the mixture into the prepared tins and smooth the surfaces. Bake in the preheated oven for 25–30 minutes, or until well risen and firm. Transfer to a wire rack to cool.

> 4

Sandwich the cakes together with chocolate spread. Decorate with the chocolate mint sticks, then warm a little of the spread and drizzle over the top. Serve.

honey & almond cake

serves 8

ingredients

150 g/5½ oz unsalted butter, plus
  extra for greasing
115 g/4 oz light muscovado sugar

175 g/6 oz clear honey
1 tbsp lemon juice
2 eggs, beaten

200 g/7 oz self-raising flour
15 g/½ oz flaked almonds
warmed honey, to glaze

> 1 Preheat the oven to 180°C/350°F/ Gas Mark 4. Grease and line a 20-cm/8-inch cake tin.

> 2 Place the butter, sugar, honey and lemon juice in a saucepan and stir over a medium heat, without boiling, until melted and smooth.

> 3 Remove the pan from the heat and gradually beat in the eggs. Sift the flour into the pan and fold into the butter mixture. Pour the mixture into the prepared tin and scatter the almonds over the top.

> 4 Bake in the preheated oven for 35–40 minutes, until well risen and firm. Transfer to a wire rack to cool. Brush with the warmed honey and serve.

orange madeira ring

serves 8

ingredients

1 tbsp golden syrup (plus extra for drizzling, if liked)

2 medium oranges

175 g/6 oz unsalted butter, plus extra for greasing

175 g/6 oz caster sugar

3 eggs, beaten

115 g/4 oz plain flour

115 g/4 oz self-raising flour

finely grated rind of 1 orange

2–3 tbsp orange juice

>1 Preheat the oven to 160 C/325 F/ Gas Mark 3. Grease a 1.5-litre/2¾-pint ring cake tin and spoon the syrup into the base.

>2 Cut all the peel and white pith from the oranges and slice. Arrange the orange slices over the syrup in the tin.

>3 Place the butter and sugar in a bowl and beat together until light and fluffy.

>4 Gradually beat in the eggs.

>5 Sift the flours into the bowl and fold into the butter mixture. Stir in orange rind and juice. Spoon the mixture into the prepared tin and smooth the surface.

>6 Bake in the preheated oven for 45–55 minutes, or until well risen and firm. Transfer to a wire rack to cool. Serve warm or cold, drizzled with additional golden syrup, if liked.

caramel peach gâteau

serves 8

ingredients

175 g/6 oz unsalted butter,
  softened, plus extra for greasing
175 g/6 oz light muscovado sugar
3 eggs, beaten

1 tsp vanilla extract
175 g/6 oz self-raising flour
½ tsp baking powder
2 tbsp milk

filling

2 tbsp maple syrup
200 ml/7 fl oz thick crème fraîche
  (40% fat)
3 ripe peaches, thinly sliced

>1 Preheat the oven to 180 C/350 F/ Gas Mark 4. Grease and base-line two 23-cm/9-inch sandwich tins.

>2 Place the butter, sugar, eggs and vanilla extract in a bowl. Sift the flour and baking powder into the bowl.

>3 Gradually beat together until smooth. Stir in the milk. Spoon the mixture into the prepared tins and smooth the surface.

>4 Bake in the preheated oven for 25–30 minutes, or until well risen and firm. Transfer to a wire rack to cool.

>5 Stir 1 tablespoon of maple syrup into the crème fraîche and spread half over each cake. Arrange half of the peach slices over one cake and top with the remaining cake, crème fraîche side down.

>6 Arrange the remaining peach slices over the top of the cake. Brush with the remaining maple syrup and serve on the day of filling.

coffee & walnut roulade

serves 6

ingredients

butter or oil, for greasing

3 eggs

1 egg white

115 g/4 oz golden caster sugar,
  plus extra for sprinkling

75 g/2¾ oz plain flour

1 tsp coffee extract

30 g finely chopped walnuts

roughly chopped walnuts,
  to decorate

filling

175 ml/6 fl oz double cream

40 g/1½ oz icing sugar, plus extra
  for dusting

1 tbsp coffee liqueur

>1 Preheat the oven to 200°C/400°F/ Gas Mark 6. Grease and line a 33 x 22-cm/13 x 8½-inch Swiss roll tin.

>2 Place the eggs, egg white and sugar in a bowl over a pan of very hot water. Beat together until thick and pale.

>3 Sift the flour into the bowl, then fold into the egg mixture. Stir in the coffee extract and walnuts. Spoon the mixture into the prepared tin and smooth the surface. Bake in the preheated oven for 12–15 minutes, or until well risen and firm.

>4 Sprinkle a sheet of baking parchment with caster sugar. Transfer the sponge to the paper and trim the edges.

>5 Roll up the sponge, from one of the short sides, with the paper inside. Leave to cool. For the filling, place the cream, sugar and liqueur in a bowl and whisk until thick.

>6 Unroll the sponge, remove the paper and spread with the cream mixture. Roll up, dust with icing sugar and sprinkle with walnuts. Serve.

apple streusel bars

makes 14 bars

ingredients

2 crisp eating apples, peeled, cored and diced

2 tbsp lemon juice

125 g/4½ oz unsalted butter, softened, plus extra for greasing

125 g/4½ oz golden caster sugar

1 tsp vanilla extract

2 eggs, beaten

150 g/5½ oz self-raising flour

topping

40 g/1½ oz blanched almonds, finely chopped

40 g/1½ oz plain flour

40 g/1½ oz light muscovado sugar

½ tsp ground cinnamon

30 g/1 oz unsalted butter, melted

Preheat the oven to 180 C/350 F/
Gas Mark 4. Grease and line a
28 x 18-cm/11 x 7-inch traybake
tin. Sprinkle the apples with
lemon juice.

Place the butter, sugar and vanilla
extract in a bowl and beat together
until light and fluffy. Gradually beat in
the eggs.

Sift the flour into the bowl, then fold
into the butter mixture. Stir in the
apples. Spoon the mixture into the
prepared tin and smooth the surface.

For the topping, mix all the ingredients
to a crumbly texture and sprinkle
over the cake mixture. Bake in the
preheated oven for 45–55 minutes, or
until well risen and firm. Cut into bars
and serve.

frosted carrot cake

serves 16

ingredients

175 ml/6 fl oz sunflower oil,
  plus extra for greasing
175 g/6 oz light muscovado sugar
3 eggs, beaten
175 g/6 oz grated carrots
85 g/3 oz sultanas
55 g/2 oz walnut pieces

grated rind of 1 orange
175 g/6 oz self-raising flour
1 tsp bicarbonate of soda
1 tsp ground cinnamon
½ tsp grated nutmeg
strips of orange zest,
  to decorate

frosting

200 g/7 oz cream cheese
100 g/3½ oz icing sugar
2 tsp orange juice

>1 Preheat the oven to 180 C/350 F/ Gas Mark 4. Grease and line a 23-cm/ 9-inch square cake tin.

>2 Place the oil, sugar and eggs in a bowl. Beat together until smooth. Stir in the carrots, sultanas, walnut pieces and orange rind.

>3 Sift the flour, bicarbonate of soda, cinnamon and nutmeg into the bowl, then fold into the carrot mixture.

>4 Spoon the mixture into the prepared tin and smooth the surface. Bake in the preheated oven for 40–45 minutes, until well risen and firm.

>5 Transfer to a wire rack to cool.

>6 For the frosting, combine the cheese, icing sugar and orange juice in a bowl and beat until smooth. Spread over the top of the cake and swirl with a palette knife. Cut into squares, decorate with strips of orange zest and serve.

cinnamon squares

makes 16 squares

ingredients

225 g/8 oz butter, softened,
   plus extra for greasing
225 g/8 oz caster sugar

3 eggs, lightly beaten
225 g/8 oz self-raising flour
½ tsp bicarbonate of soda

1 tbsp ground cinnamon
150 ml/5 fl oz soured cream
55 g/2 oz sunflower seeds

> **1** Preheat the oven to 180°C/350°F/ Gas Mark 4. Grease and line a 23-cm/9-inch square cake tin.

> **2** Place the butter and sugar in a bowl and beat together until light and fluffy. Gradually beat in the eggs.

> **3** Sift the flour, bicarbonate of soda and cinnamon into the bowl, then fold into the butter mixture. Stir in the soured cream and sunflower seeds. Spoon into the prepared tin and smooth the surface.

> **4** Bake in the preheated oven for about 45 minutes, until well risen and firm. Transfer to a wire rack to cool. Cut into squares and serve.

chocolate chip brownies

makes 12 brownies

ingredients

150 g/5½ oz plain chocolate, broken into pieces

225 g/8 oz butter, softened, plus extra for greasing

225 g/8 oz self-raising flour

125 g/4½ oz caster sugar

4 eggs, beaten

75 g/2¾ oz pistachio nuts

100 g/3½ oz white chocolate, roughly chopped

icing sugar, for dusting

>1 Preheat the oven to 180°C/350°F/ Gas Mark 4. Grease and line a 23-cm/ 9-inch square baking tin.

>2 Place the plain chocolate and butter in a bowl over a pan of very hot water. Stir until melted, then set aside to cool.

>3 Sift the flour into a separate bowl and stir in the caster sugar. Stir the eggs into the chocolate mixture, then pour into the flour and sugar and beat well.

>4 Stir in the nuts and white chocolate. Spoon the mixture into the prepared tin and smooth the surface.

>5 Bake in the preheated oven for 30–35 minutes, or until firm to the touch around the edges. Cool in the tin for 20 minutes, then turn out onto a wire rack to cool completely.

>6 Dust with icing sugar, cut into squares and serve.

pastries

cinnamon swirls 39
chocolate filo parcels 41
strawberry éclairs 43
summer fruit tartlets 45
cherry & cinnamon tartlets 47
baklava 49
chocolate nut strudel 51
lemon meringue pie 53
apple pie 55
broccoli, pancetta & blue cheese galette 57
asparagus & prosciutto wraps 59
tomato tarte tatin 61

cinnamon swirls

makes 12 swirls

ingredients

225 g/8 oz strong white flour

½ tsp salt

7 g/¼ oz easy-blend dried yeast

25 g/1 oz butter, cut into small
  pieces, plus extra for greasing

1 egg, lightly beaten

125 ml/4 fl oz lukewarm milk

2 tbsp maple syrup, for glazing

filling

55 g/2 oz butter, softened

2 tsp ground cinnamon

50 g/1¾ oz soft light brown sugar

50 g/1¾ oz currants

> 1 Grease a baking sheet and a bowl. Sift the flour and salt into a separate bowl and stir in the yeast.

> 2 Place the butter in the bowl with the flour. Rub together until the mixture resembles breadcrumbs. Add the egg and milk and mix to form a dough. Form the dough into a ball, place in the greased bowl, cover and leave in a warm place for 40 minutes, or until doubled in volume.

> 3 Punch down the dough lightly for 1 minute, then roll out to a rectangle measuring 30 x 23 cm/12 x 19 inches.

> 4 For the filling, beat together the softened butter, cinnamon and sugar until light and fluffy. Spread the filling over the dough, leaving a 2.5-cm/1-inch border. Sprinkle the currants evenly over the top. Roll up the dough from one of the long edges and press down to seal.

> 5 Preheat the oven to 190°C/375°F/Gas Mark 5. Cut the roll into twelve slices and place them on the prepared baking sheet. Cover and leave to stand for 30 minutes.

> 6 Bake in the preheated oven for 20–30 minutes, or until well risen. Brush with maple syrup and leave to cool slightly before serving.

chocolate filo parcels

makes 18 parcels

ingredients

85 g/3 oz ground hazelnuts
1 tbsp finely chopped fresh mint
125 ml/4 fl oz soured cream
2 eating apples, peeled and
  grated
55 g/2 oz plain chocolate, melted

9 sheets filo pastry, about
  15 cm/6 inches square
55–85 g/2–3 oz butter, melted, plus
  extra for greasing
icing sugar, for dusting

>1 Preheat the oven to 190°C/375°F/ Gas Mark 5. Grease a baking sheet. Place the nuts, mint and soured cream in a bowl and beat together until well combined. Stir in the apples and chocolate.

>2 Cut each pastry sheet into four squares. Brush one square with butter, then place a second square on top and brush with the melted butter.

>3 Place 1 tablespoon of the chocolate mixture in the centre, bring up the corners and twist together. Repeat until all of the pastry and filling has been used.

>4 Place the parcels on the prepared baking sheet and bake in the preheated oven for 10 minutes, or until crisp and golden. Remove from the oven and leave to cool slightly. Dust with icing sugar and serve.

strawberry éclairs

makes 16 éclairs

ingredients

55 g/2 oz unsalted butter,
  plus extra for greasing
150 ml/5 fl oz water
8 tbsp plain flour
2 eggs, beaten

filling

200 g/7 oz strawberries,
  finely chopped
2 tbsp icing sugar
140 g/5 oz mascarpone cheese

Preheat the oven to 220°C/425°F/ Gas Mark 7. Grease two baking sheets. Heat the butter and water in a saucepan until boiling.

Remove the pan from the heat, sift in the flour and beat together until smooth. Transfer to a bowl.

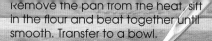

>3

Gradually beat in the eggs with an electric hand mixer, until glossy.

>4

Spoon into a piping bag with a large plain nozzle and pipe eighteen 9-cm/3½-inch fingers on the prepared baking sheets.

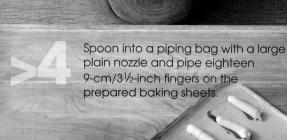

>5

Bake in the preheated oven for 12–15 minutes, until well risen. Cut a slit down the side of each éclair to release steam. Bake for a further 2 minutes. Transfer to a wire rack to cool.

>6

Purée half of the strawberries with the icing sugar and set aside. Stir the remaining strawberries into the mascarpone and pipe the mixture into the éclairs. Serve with the strawberry purée, preferably within an hour of filling.

summer fruit tartlets

makes 12 tartlets

ingredients

200 g/7 oz plain flour, plus extra for
   dusting
85 g/3 oz icing sugar
55 g/2 oz ground almonds

115 g/4 oz butter
1 tbsp milk
1 egg yolk

filling

225 g/8 oz cream cheese
icing sugar, to taste, plus extra
   for dusting
350 g/12 oz fresh summer berries

>1 Sift the flour and icing sugar into a bowl. Stir in the almonds. Add the butter and rub together until the mixture resembles breadcrumbs. Add the milk and egg yolk and mix to form a soft dough. Wrap the dough in clingfilm and chill for 30 minutes.

>2 Preheat the oven to 200°C/400°F/ Gas Mark 6. Roll out the dough on a lightly floured surface and use it to line twelve deep tartlet tins. Prick the bases and press a piece of foil into each.

>3 Bake in the preheated oven for 10–15 minutes, or until light golden brown. Remove the foil and bake for a further 2–3 minutes. Transfer to a wire rack to cool.

>4 For the filling, place the cream cheese and icing sugar in a bowl and mix together. Place a spoonful of the mixture in each tartlet and arrange the berries on top. Dust with icing sugar and serve.

cherry & cinnamon tartlets

makes 4 tartlets

ingredients

125 g/4½ oz plain flour
2 tbsp icing sugar
½ tsp ground cinnamon
70 g/2½ oz unsalted butter, at
   room temperature

1 egg yolk
2 tbsp cold water

filling

350 g/12 oz cherries, pitted
150 ml/5 fl oz Greek-style yogurt
2 tbsp clear honey
cinnamon and whole cherries, to
   decorate

>1 Preheat the oven to 190°C/375°F/
Gas Mark 5. Place the flour, icing
sugar, cinnamon and butter in a
food processor and process until
evenly blended.

>2 Add the egg yolk and water to the
mixture, and mix to form a soft dough.

>3 Divide the pastry into four and press
into four 18-cm/4-inch loose-based
tartlet tins. Prick the bases and press
a piece of foil into each. Bake in the
preheated oven for 12–15 minutes
or until light and golden brown.
Remove the foil and bake for a
further 2–3 minutes.

>4 Transfer to a wire rack to cool. To
make the filling, stir the pitted cherries
into the yogurt and spoon into the
cases. Drizzle with honey, sprinkle
with cinnamon and serve with whole
cherries.

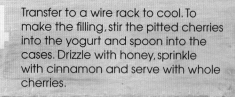

baklava

serves 16

ingredients

225 g/8 oz walnut halves, finely
  chopped
225 g/8 oz shelled pistachio nuts,
  finely chopped
100 g/3½ oz blanched almonds,
  finely chopped
4 tbsp pine nuts, finely chopped
finely grated rind of 2 large
  oranges

6 tbsp sesame seeds
1 tbsp sugar
½ tsp ground cinnamon
½ tsp mixed spice
250 g/9 oz butter, melted, plus extra
  for greasing
23 sheets filo pastry

syrup

450 g/1 lb caster sugar
450 ml/16 fl oz water
5 tbsp honey
3 cloves

>1 Place the walnuts, pistachios, almonds and pine nuts in a bowl and stir in the orange rind, sesame seeds, sugar, cinnamon and mixed spice.

>2 Preheat the oven to 160°C/325°F/ Gas Mark 3. Grease a 25-cm/ 10-inch square ovenproof dish with a little of the butter. Stack the pastry sheets and cut to the size of the dish using a ruler.

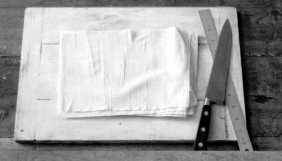

>3 Place a sheet of pastry on the base of the dish and brush with melted butter. Top with seven more sheets, brushing with butter between each layer.

>4 Sprinkle with a generous 150 g/5½ oz of the filling. Top with three sheets of pastry, brushing each one with butter. Continue until you have used all the pastry and filling, ending with a top layer of three sheets.

>5 Brush the top pastry layer with butter. Cut into 5-cm/2-inch squares. Brush again with butter. Bake in the preheated oven for 1 hour.

>6 To make the syrup, place all the ingredients in a saucepan. Slowly bring to the boil, stirring to dissolve the sugar, then simmer for 15 minutes. Remove from the heat and leave to cool. Strain the syrup over the baklava and leave to cool. Cut into squares and serve.

chocolate nut strudel

serves 6

ingredients

200 g/7 oz mixed chopped nuts
115 g/4 oz plain chocolate, chopped
115 g/4 oz milk chocolate, chopped

115 g/4 oz white chocolate, chopped
200 g/7 oz filo pastry
150 g/5½ oz unsalted butter, melted, plus extra for greasing

3 tbsp golden syrup
55 g/2 oz icing sugar, for dusting

...heat the oven to 190°C/375°F/
Gas Mark 5. Grease a baking sheet.
Reserve 1 tablespoon of the nuts.
Place the remaining nuts in a
bowl with the chocolate and
stir to combine.

2

Place a sheet of pastry on a clean
tea towel. Brush with butter, drizzle with
golden syrup and sprinkle with the nut
and chocolate mixture. Place another
sheet on top and repeat the process
until you have used all the nuts and
chocolate.

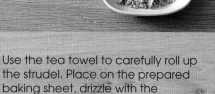

>3 Use the tea towel to carefully roll up
the strudel. Place on the prepared
baking sheet, drizzle with the
remaining golden syrup and
sprinkle with the reserved nuts.

>4 Bake in the preheated oven for
20–25 minutes. If the nuts start to
brown too much, cover with a sheet
of foil. Dust the strudel with icing sugar,
slice and serve.

lemon meringue pie

serves 8

ingredients

150 g/5½ oz plain flour, plus extra
   for dusting
85 g/3 oz butter, cut into small
   pieces, plus extra for greasing

35 g/1¼ oz icing sugar
finely grated rind of ½ lemon
½ egg yolk, beaten
1½ tbsp milk

filling

3 tbsp cornflour
300 ml/10 fl oz water
juice and grated rind of
   2 lemons
175 g/6 oz caster sugar
2 eggs, separated

>1 Sift the flour into a bowl. Add the butter and rub together until the mixture resembles breadcrumbs. Add the icing sugar, lemon rind, egg yolk and milk and mix to form a dough.

>2 Knead briefly on a lightly floured surface. Wrap the dough in clingfilm and chill for 30 minutes.

>3 Preheat the oven to 180°C/350°F/ Gas Mark 4. Grease a 20-cm/8-inch round tart tin. Roll out the pastry to 5 mm/¼ inch thick, then use it to line the tin. Prick the base all over with a fork, line with baking paper and fill with baking beans. Bake in the preheated oven for 15 minutes, or until light golden brown.

>4 Remove from the oven and take out the paper and baking beans. Reduce the oven temperature to 150°C/300°F/ Gas Mark 2.

>5 For the filling, mix the cornflour with a little water to form a paste. Put the remaining water in a saucepan. Add the lemon juice and rind and the cornflour paste to the pan. Bring to the boil, stirring. Cook for 2 minutes. Cool slightly. Stir in 5 tablespoons of the caster sugar and the egg yolks, and pour into the pastry case.

>6 Whisk the egg whites in a clean, grease-free bowl until stiff. Gradually whisk in the remaining caster sugar and spread over the pie. Place on a baking sheet and bake for 40 minutes. Remove from the oven and cool. Serve.

54

apple pie

serves 8

ingredients

350 g/12 oz plain flour

pinch of salt

85 g/3 oz butter, cut into pieces

85 g/3 oz lard, cut into small pieces

1–2 tbsp water

beaten egg or milk, for glazing

filling

750 g–1 kg/1 lb 10 oz–2 lb 4 oz
    cooking apples, peeled, cored
    and sliced

125 g/4½ oz soft light brown sugar,
    plus extra for sprinkling

½–1 tsp ground cinnamon

>1 ...the flour and salt into a bowl. Add the butter and lard, and rub together until the mixture resembles breadcrumbs. Add the water, a little at a time, and mix to form a firm dough.

>2 Wrap the dough in clingfilm and chill for 30 minutes. Preheat the oven to 220°C/425°F/Gas Mark 7. Roll out two thirds of the pastry and use to line a 23-cm/9-inch pie dish.

>3 For the filling, mix the apples with the sugar and cinnamon, and pack into the pastry case.

>4 Roll out the remaining pastry to form a lid. Dampen the edges of the pie rim with water and position the lid, pressing the edges firmly together. Trim and crimp the edges. Use the pastry trimmings to cut out leaves or other shapes. Dampen and attach to the top of the pie.

>5 Glaze the pie with beaten egg or milk, make one or two slits in the top and place the pie on a baking sheet.

>6 Bake in the preheated oven for 20 minutes, then reduce the temperature to 180°C/350°F/Gas Mark 4 and bake for a further 30 minutes, or until the pastry is golden brown. Sprinkle with sugar and serve hot or cold.

broccoli, pancetta & blue cheese galette

serves 4

ingredients

1 sheet ready-rolled puff pastry
(half a pack)

225 g/8 oz small broccoli florets,
halved if necessary

125 g/4½ oz diced pancetta

1 small red onion, sliced

100 g/3½ oz Gorgonzola or
Roquefort cheese, chopped

ground black pepper

toasted pine nuts, to garnish

>1 Preheat the oven to 200°C/400°C/ Gas Mark 6. Place the pastry on a baking sheet and lightly score a line all around, cutting only halfway through, 1 cm/½ inch from the edge.

>2 Steam or boil the broccoli for 4–5 minutes, until just tender. Drain.

>3 Fry the pancetta with the onion, stirring, until golden. Stir in the broccoli and season with black pepper.

>4 Spread the filling over the pastry, leaving the border clear.

>5 Scatter the pieces of cheese evenly over the top.

>6 Bake in the preheated oven for 25–30 minutes, until the pastry is risen and golden. Sprinkle with toasted pine nuts and serve warm.

asparagus & prosciutto wraps

makes 6 wraps

ingredients

225 g/8 oz asparagus, trimmed

375 g/13 oz pack ready-rolled
  chilled puff pastry sheet

2 tbsp pesto

6 thin slices prosciutto

85 g/3 oz grated Emmental
  cheese

milk, for glazing

ground black pepper

>1 Preheat the oven to 220°C/425°F/ Gas Mark 7. Cook the asparagus in boiling water for 5–6 minutes, until tender. Drain.

>2 Cut the pastry into six squares. Place on a baking sheet and spread 1 teaspoon of pesto on the centre of each.

>3 Divide the asparagus into six bunches and wrap each in a prosciutto slice. Place diagonally on each square and top with grated cheese and pepper.

>4 Lift opposite corners over to meet on top, brushing with milk to glaze. Bake in the preheated oven for 15–20 minutes, until golden brown. Serve the wraps warm or cold.

tomato tarte tatin

serves 4

ingredients

25 g/1 oz butter

1 tbsp caster sugar

500 g/1 lb 2 oz cherry tomatoes, halved

1 clove garlic, crushed

2 tsp white wine vinegar

salt and pepper

pastry

250 g/9 oz plain flour

pinch of salt

140 g/5 oz butter

1 tbsp chopped oregano, plus extra to garnish

5–6 tbsp cold water

>1 Preheat the oven to 200°C/400°F/Gas Mark 6. Melt the butter in a heavy-based pan. Add the sugar and stir over a fairly high heat until just turning golden brown.

>2 Remove from the heat and quickly add the tomatoes, garlic and white wine vinegar, stirring to coat evenly. Season with salt and pepper.

>3 Place the tomatoes in a 23-cm/9-inch cake tin, spreading evenly.

>4 For the pastry, place the flour, salt, butter and oregano in a food processor and process until the mixture resembles breadcrumbs. Add the water, a little at a time, and mix to form a soft, but not sticky, dough.

>5 Roll out the pastry to a 25-cm/10-inch round and place over the tomatoes, tucking in the edges. Pierce with a fork to let out steam.

>6 Bake in the preheated oven for 25–30 minutes, until golden brown. Rest for 2–3 minutes, then run a knife around the edge and turn out onto a warmed serving plate. Sprinkle with chopped oregano and serve warm.

small cakes & biscuits

chocolate butterfly cupcakes

makes 12 cupcakes

ingredients

125 g/4½ oz soft margarine
125 g/4½ oz caster sugar
150 g/5½ oz self-raising flour

2 large eggs
2 tbsp cocoa powder
25 g/1 oz plain chocolate, melted

lemon buttercream

100 g/3½ oz unsalted butter,
  softened
225 g/8 oz icing sugar, plus extra
  for dusting
grated rind of ½ lemon
1 tbsp lemon juice

> 1 Preheat the oven to 180°C/350°F/ Gas Mark 4. Place twelve paper cases in a bun tin.

> 2 Place the margarine, caster sugar, flour, eggs and cocoa powder in a bowl and beat together until smooth. Stir in the melted chocolate.

> 3 Spoon the mixture into the paper cases, filling them three-quarters full.

> 4 Bake in the preheated oven for 15 minutes, or until well risen. Transfer to a wire rack to cool.

> 5 For the buttercream, place the butter in a bowl and beat until fluffy. Gradually beat in the icing sugar, lemon rind and lemon juice.

> 6 Cut the top off each cake, using a serrated knife. Cut each cake top in half. Spread the buttercream over the cut surface of each cake and push the two pieces of cake top into the icing to form wings. Dust with icing sugar and serve.

frosted peanut butter cupcakes

makes 16 cupcakes

ingredients

55 g/2 oz butter, softened
225 g/8 oz soft light brown sugar
115 g/4 oz crunchy peanut butter
2 eggs, lightly beaten

1 tsp vanilla extract
225 g/8 oz plain white flour
2 tsp baking powder
100 ml/3½ fl oz milk

frosting

200 g/7 oz cream cheese
25 g/1 oz butter, softened
225 g/8 oz icing sugar

>1 Preheat the oven to 180°C/350°F/ Gas Mark 4. Place sixteen double-layer paper cases on a baking sheet.

>2 Place the butter, sugar and peanut butter in a bowl and beat together until well combined. Gradually beat in the eggs and the vanilla extract.

>3 Sift the flour and baking powder into the bowl, then fold into the butter mixture. Stir in the milk.

>4 Spoon the mixture into the paper cases, filling them three-quarters full. Bake in the preheated oven for 25 minutes, or until well risen. Transfer to a wire rack to cool.

>5 For the frosting, place the cream cheese and butter in a bowl and beat together until smooth. Gradually beat in the icing sugar.

>6 When the cupcakes are cold, spread some frosting on top of each, swirling with a round-bladed knife. Store in the refrigerator until ready to serve.

fairy cupcakes

makes 16 cupcakes

ingredients

115 g/4 oz unsalted butter

115 g/4 oz caster sugar

2 eggs, beaten

115 g/4 oz self-raising flour

sugar flowers, hundreds and
thousands, glacé cherries and/or
chocolate strands, to decorate

icing

200 g/7 oz icing sugar

about 2 tbsp lukewarm water

food colourings (optional)

>1 Preheat the oven to 180°C/350°F/ Gas Mark 4. Put sixteen double-layer paper cases on a baking sheet.

>2 Place the butter and caster sugar in a large bowl and beat together until light and fluffy. Gradually beat in the eggs. Sift the flour into the bowl, then fold into the butter mixture.

>3 Spoon the mixture into the paper cases, filling them three-quarters full. Bake in the preheated oven for 15–20 minutes, or until well risen. Transfer to a wire rack to cool.

>4 For the icing, sift the icing sugar into a bowl, then add enough water to mix to a thick, smooth paste. Stir in a few drops of food colouring, if using, then spread over the cakes. Decorate with sugar flowers, hundreds and thousands and glacé cherries, and serve.

double ginger cupcakes

makes 12 cupcakes

ingredients

175 g/6 oz plain flour

1 tbsp baking powder

2 tsp ground ginger

175 g/6 oz unsalted butter,
  softened

175 g/6 oz light muscovado sugar

3 eggs, beaten

25 g/1 oz crystallized stem ginger,
  finely chopped

frosting

200 g/7 oz ricotta cheese

85 g/3 oz icing sugar

finely grated rind 1 tangerine

diced crystallized ginger,
  to decorate

>1 Preheat the oven to 190°C/375°F/ Gas Mark 5. Place twelve paper cases in a bun tin.

>2 Sift the flour, baking powder and ground ginger into a bowl.

>3 Add the butter, muscovado sugar and eggs and beat together until smooth. Stir in the crystallized ginger.

>4 Spoon the mixture into the paper cases, filling them three-quarters full. Bake in the preheated oven for 15–20 minutes, or until well risen. Transfer to a wire rack to cool.

>5 For the frosting, place the ricotta, icing sugar and tangerine rind in a bowl and beat together until smooth.

>6 Spoon a little frosting onto each cake and spread over the surface to cover. Decorate with diced crystallized ginger and serve.

apricot, macadamia & white chocolate muffins

makes 12 muffins

ingredients

280 g/10 oz plain flour
1 tbsp baking powder
115 g/4 oz golden caster sugar
85 g/3 oz ready to eat dried
   apricots, chopped

55 g/2 oz macadamia nuts,
   chopped
55 g/2 oz white chocolate,
   chopped
2 eggs, beaten

200 ml/7 fl oz buttermilk
100 ml/3½ fl oz sunflower oil

>1 Preheat the oven to 200°C/400°F/ Gas Mark 6. Place twelve paper cases in a muffin tray.

>2 Sift the flour and baking powder into a bowl and stir in the sugar, apricots, nuts and chocolate.

>3 Place the eggs, buttermilk and oil in a jug and beat together. Add to the flour mixture and stir until well combined.

>4 Spoon the mixture into the paper cases, filling them three-quarters full. Bake in the preheated oven for 20–25 minutes, or until well risen. Serve the muffins warm, preferably on the day of making.

blueberry muffins

makes 12 muffins

ingredients

225 g/8 oz plain flour
1 tsp bicarbonate of soda
¼ tsp salt
1 tsp ground allspice

115 g/4 oz caster sugar
3 large egg whites
3 tbsp low-fat margarine
150 ml/5 fl oz natural yogurt

1 tsp vanilla extract
85 g/3 oz fresh blueberries

> 1

Preheat the oven to 190°C/375°F/ Gas Mark 5. Place twelve paper cases in a muffin tray.

> 2

Sift the flour, bicarbonate of soda, salt and half the allspice into a bowl. Add 6 tablespoons of the sugar and stir to combine.

> 3

In a separate bowl, whisk the egg whites together. Stir in the margarine, yogurt, vanilla extract and blueberries.

> 4

Add the egg mixture to the flour mixture and fold together until loosely combined – it is fine for the mixture to be a little lumpy.

> 5

Spoon the mixture into the paper cases, filling them three-quarters full. Mix the remaining sugar with the remaining allspice and sprinkle over the muffins.

> 6

Bake in the preheated oven for 25 minutes, or until well risen. Transfer to a wire rack to cool. Serve warm or cool.

classic oatmeal biscuits

makes 10–20 biscuits

ingredients

175 g/6 oz butter or margarine,
 plus extra for greasing
275 g/9¾ oz demerara sugar
1 egg

4 tbsp water
1 tsp vanilla extract
375 g/13 oz rolled oats
140 g/5 oz plain flour

1 tsp salt
½ tsp bicarbonate of soda

> 1

Preheat the oven to 350°F / 180°C / Gas Mark 4 and grease a large baking sheet.

> 2

Place the butter and sugar in a bowl and beat together until light and fluffy. Gradually beat in the egg, water and vanilla extract until smooth.

> 3

In a separate bowl, mix the oats, flour, salt and bicarbonate of soda. Gradually stir the oat mixture into the butter mixture until thoroughly combined.

> 4

Place well-spaced tablespoonfuls of the mixture onto the prepared baking tray. Bake in the preheated oven for 15 minutes, or until golden brown. Remove from the oven and cool on a wire rack. For a sweeter option, drizzle with melted chocolate.

chocolate chip cookies

makes 8 cookies

ingredients

unsalted butter, melted,
   for greasing
175 g/6 oz plain flour, sifted
1 tsp baking powder

125 g/4½ oz margarine
85 g/3 oz light muscovado sugar
55 g/2 oz caster sugar
½ tsp vanilla extract

1 egg
125 g/4½ oz plain chocolate chips

>1 ...heat the oven to 190°C/375°F/
Gas Mark 5. Line and lightly grease
two baking sheets.

>2 Place all of the ingredients in
a large mixing bowl and beat
until well combined.

>3 Place well-spaced tablespoonfuls
of the <u>mixture</u> onto the prepared
baking trays.

>4 Bake in the preheated oven for
10–12 minutes, or until golden brown.
Transfer to a wire rack to cool. Serve,
or store in an airtight container for up
to two weeks.

mini florentines

makes 20–30 florentines

ingredients

75 g/2¾ oz butter

75 g/2¾ oz caster sugar

25 g/1 oz sultanas or raisins

25 g/1 oz glacé cherries, chopped

25 g/1 oz crystallized stem ginger, finely chopped

25 g/1 oz sunflower seeds

100 g/3½ oz flaked almonds

2 tbsp double cream

175 g/6 oz plain or milk chocolate, broken into pieces

>1 Preheat the oven to 180°C/350°F/Gas Mark 4. Line two baking sheets. Place the butter in a small saucepan and melt over a low heat. Add the sugar, stir until dissolved, then bring to the boil.

>2 Remove from the heat and stir in the sultanas, glacé cherries, crystallized ginger, sunflower seeds and almonds. Mix well, then beat in the cream.

>3 Place small, well-spaced teaspoons of mixture onto the prepared baking trays. Bake in the preheated oven for 10–12 minutes, or until light golden in colour.

>4 Remove from the oven and, while still hot, use a circular biscuit cutter to tidy the edges of the florentines. Pile any excess mixture on top of the circles. Leave to cool before removing from the baking sheets.

>5 Put the chocolate in a heatproof bowl set over a saucepan of gently simmering water and stir until melted. Spread most of the chocolate onto a sheet of baking paper. When the chocolate is on the point of setting, place the biscuits flat-side down on the chocolate and let it harden completely.

>6 Cut around the florentines and remove from the baking paper. Spread the remaining chocolate on the coated side of the florentines, using a fork to mark waves. Leave to set.

chocolate hazelnut flapjack cookies

makes 16 cookies

ingredients

85 g/3 oz unsalted butter, plus extra
  for greasing
175 g/6 oz chocolate hazelnut
  spread

175 g/6 oz porridge oats
70 g/2½ oz blanched hazelnuts,
  chopped

>1 Preheat the oven to 200°C/400°F/ Gas Mark 6. Grease a baking sheet.

>2 Place the butter and chocolate spread in a pan and heat gently until just melted.

>3 Add the porridge oats and hazelnuts to the chocolate mixture and stir to combine thoroughly.

>4 Shape the mixture into sixteen equal-size balls, then press onto the prepared baking sheet. Bake in the preheated oven for 10–12 minutes, remove from the oven and leave for a 3–4 minutes, or until firm. Transfer to a wire rack to cool. Serve, or store in an airtight container for up to two weeks.

cranberry & pine nut biscotti

makes 18–20 biscotti

ingredients

butter or oil, for greasing

85 g/3 oz light muscovado sugar

1 large egg

140 g/5 oz plain flour

½ tsp baking powder

1 tsp ground allspice

55 g/2 oz dried cranberries

55 g/2 oz pine nuts, toasted

>1 Preheat the oven to 180°C/350°F/ Gas Mark 4. Grease a baking sheet. Whisk together the sugar and egg, until pale and thick. Sift the flour, baking powder and allspice into the bowl, and fold into the egg mixture.

>2 Stir in the cranberries and pine nuts and mix to form a smooth dough.

>3 With lightly floured hands, shape the mixture into a long roll, about 28 cm/ 11 inches long. Press to flatten slightly.

>4 Lift the dough onto the baking sheet and bake in the preheated oven for 20–25 minutes, until golden.

>5 Cool for 3–4 minutes, then cut into 1.5-cm/⅝-inch thick slices and arrange on the baking sheet.

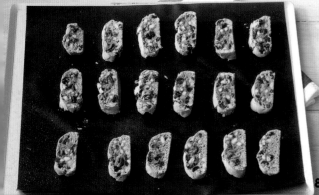

>6 Bake in the oven for 10 minutes, or until golden brown. Transfer to a wire rack to cool. Serve, or store in an airtight container for up to three weeks.

marzipan whirls

makes 8 whirls

ingredients

125 g/4½ oz unsalted butter,
  softened
30 g/1 oz caster sugar

½ tsp almond essence
125 g/4½ oz plain flour
1 tbsp milk, to mix

40 g/1½ oz almond paste
4 tsp apricot jam, warmed
icing sugar, for dusting

>1 [Preheat the oven to 1?0 C, 375 F,]
Gas Mark 5. Place eight paper cases in a bun tin. Place the butter, caster sugar and almond essence in a food processor and process until pale and fluffy.

>2 [Stir] in the flour and process to a soft dough, adding milk if necessary. Spoon the mixture into a piping bag fitted with a large star nozzle.

>3 Pipe the mixture in a spiral around the sides of each case, leaving a dip in the centre.

>4 Cut the almond paste into 8 cubes and press one into the centre of each whirl.

>5 Bake in the preheated oven for 15–20 minutes, until pale and golden. Transfer to a wire rack to cool.

>6 Once cooled, spoon a little of the apricot jam into the centre of each cake. Dust with icing sugar and serve.

lemon & poppy seed madeleines

makes 30 madeleines

ingredients

oil, for greasing

3 eggs

1 egg yolk

finely grated rind of 1 lemon

140 g/5 oz golden caster sugar

140 g/5 oz plain flour

1 tsp baking powder

140 g/5 oz unsalted butter, melted
  and cooled

1 tbsp poppy seeds

> **1** Preheat the oven to 190°C/375°F/ Gas Mark 5. Lightly grease three twelve-hole madeleine tins.

> **2** Whisk the eggs, yolk, lemon rind and sugar in a large bowl until very pale and thick.

> **3** Sift the flour and baking powder over the egg mixture and fold in lightly using a metal spoon. Fold in the melted butter and poppy seeds.

> **4** Spoon the mixture into the tins and bake in the preheated oven for about 10 minutes, until well risen. Transfer to a wire rack to cool. Serve.

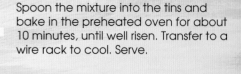

breads

crusty white bread

makes 1 loaf

ingredients

1 egg
1 egg yolk
150–200 ml/5–7 fl oz lukewarm
  water

500 g/1 lb 2 oz strong white flour,
  sifted, plus extra for dusting
1½ tsp salt
2 tsp sugar

1 tsp easy-blend dried yeast
25 g/1 oz butter, diced
oil, for greasing

>1 Place the egg and egg yolk in a jug and beat lightly to mix. Add enough water to make up to 300 ml/10 fl oz. Stir well.

>2 Place the flour, salt, sugar and yeast in a bowl. Add the butter and rub together until the mixture resembles breadcrumbs. Add the egg mixture and mix to form a dough. Turn out onto a lightly floured surface and knead well for about 10 minutes, until smooth and elastic.

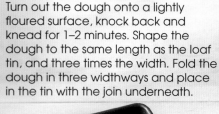

>3 Grease a bowl and a 900-g/2-lb loaf tin. Form the dough into a ball, place in the greased bowl, cover and leave in a warm place for 1 hour, or until doubled in volume. Preheat the oven to 220°C/425°F/Gas Mark 7.

>4 Turn out the dough onto a lightly floured surface, knock back and knead for 1–2 minutes. Shape the dough to the same length as the loaf tin, and three times the width. Fold the dough in three widthways and place in the tin with the join underneath.

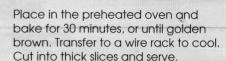

>5 Cover and leave in a warm place for 30 minutes, until the dough has risen above the tin.

>6 Place in the preheated oven and bake for 30 minutes, or until golden brown. Transfer to a wire rack to cool. Cut into thick slices and serve.

plaited poppy seed bread

makes 1 loaf

ingredients

225 g/8 oz strong white flour, plus
  extra for dusting
1 tsp salt
2 tbsp skimmed milk powder
1½ tbsp caster sugar

1 tsp easy-blend dried yeast
175 ml/6 fl oz lukewarm water
2 tbsp vegetable oil, plus extra for
  greasing
5 tbsp poppy seeds

topping

1 egg yolk
1 tbsp milk
1 tbsp caster sugar
2 tbsp poppy seeds

>1 Sift the flour and salt into a bowl and stir in the milk powder, sugar and yeast. Add the water and oil and mix to form a dough.

>2 Add the poppy seeds and knead until well combined. Turn out the dough onto a lightly floured surface and knead for about 10 minutes, until smooth and elastic.

>3 Grease a bowl and a baking sheet. Form the dough into a ball, place in the greased bowl, cover and leave in a warm place for 1 hour, or until doubled in volume.

>4 Turn out the dough onto a lightly floured surface, knock back and knead for 1–2 minutes. Divide into three equal pieces and shape each into a rope 25-30 cm/10–12 inches long. Plait the dough, press each end together and tuck underneath.

>5 Place the loaf on the prepared baking sheet, cover and leave to rise in a warm place for 30 minutes. Meanwhile, preheat the oven to 200°C/400°F/Gas Mark 6.

>6 For the topping, beat the egg yolk with the milk and sugar. Brush the egg glaze over the top of the loaf and sprinkle with the poppy seeds. Bake in the preheated oven for 30–35 minutes, until golden brown. Transfer to a wire rack to cool.

irish soda bread

makes 1 loaf

ingredients

butter, melted, for greasing

450 g/1 lb plain flour, plus extra for
   dusting

1 tsp salt

1 tsp bicarbonate of soda

400 ml/14 fl oz buttermilk

> **1** Preheat the oven to 220°C/425°F/ Gas Mark 7. Lightly grease a baking sheet.

> **2** Sift the flour, salt and bicarbonate of soda into a bowl. Add three quarters of the buttermilk and mix to form a soft dough. Add the remaining buttermilk, if necessary.

> **3** Turn out the dough onto a floured surface and knead. Shape into a 20-cm/8-inch round.

> **4** Place the bread on the prepared baking sheet, cut a cross in the top and bake in the preheated oven for 25–30 minutes. Transfer to a wire rack to cool.

rye bread

makes 1 loaf

ingredients

450 g/1 lb rye flour

225 g/8 oz strong white flour,
  plus extra for dusting

2 tsp salt

2 tsp soft light brown sugar

1½ tsp easy-blend dried yeast

425 ml/15 fl oz lukewarm water

2 tsp vegetable oil, plus extra for
  greasing

1 egg white

>1 Grease a bowl and a baking sheet. Sift the flours and salt together into a separate bowl. Stir in the sugar and yeast. Add the water and oil and mix to form a dough.

>2 Turn out the dough onto a lightly floured surface and knead for 10 minutes, until smooth and elastic. Shape the dough into a ball, place in the greased bowl, cover and leave in a warm place for 2 hours, or until doubled in volume.

>3 Turn out the dough onto a lightly floured surface, knockback and knead for 10 minutes.

>4 Form the dough into a ball, put it on the prepared baking tray and cover. Leave to rise in a warm place for a further 40 minutes, or until doubled in volume. Meanwhile, preheat the oven to 190°C/375°F/Gas Mark 5. Beat the egg white with 1 tablespoon of water in a bowl.

>5 Bake the loaf in the preheated oven for 20 minutes, then remove from the oven and brush the top with the egg white glaze.

>6 Return to the oven for a further 20–30 minutes, until golden brown. Transfer to a wire rack to cool.

pumpkin &
seed twist

makes 1 loaf

ingredients

250 g/9 oz peeled pumpkin, diced

1 tsp fennel seeds

grated rind of 1 lemon

2 tbsp clear honey

500 g/1lb 2 oz strong plain flour

½ tsp salt

6 g sachet easy-blend dried yeast

300 ml/10 fl oz lukewarm water

oil, for greasing

milk, for glazing

2 tbsp pumpkin and sunflower
  seeds

>1 Grease a bowl and a baking sheet. Steam the pumpkin for 10 minutes or until tender. Drain thoroughly. Mash the pumpkin and stir in the fennel seeds, lemon rind and honey.

>2 Sift the flour and salt into a bowl and stir in the yeast. Add the pumpkin mixture, then the water, a little at a time, and mix to form a soft dough. Turn out the dough onto a lightly floured surface and knead for 10 minutes, until smooth and elastic.

>3 Form the dough into a ball, place in the greased bowl, cover and leave in a warm place for 30 minutes, or until doubled in volume.

>4 Divide into two equal pieces and shape each into a rope 35 cm/14 inches long. Twist the ropes together, press each end together and tuck underneath. Place on the prepared baking sheet, cover and leave in a warm place for 1–1½ hours, or until doubled in volume.

>5 Preheat the oven to 200°C/400°F/ Gas Mark 6. Brush the loaf with milk and sprinkle with pumpkin and sunflower seeds.

>6 Bake in the preheated oven for 30–35 minutes, or until golden. It should sound hollow when tapped underneath. Transfer to a wire rack to cool.

spring onion & parmesan cornbread

serves 16

ingredients

oil, for greasing
140 g/5 oz fine cornmeal
140 g/5 oz plain flour
4 tsp baking powder

2 tsp celery salt
55 g/2 oz Parmesan cheese, grated
2 eggs, beaten

400 ml/14 fl oz milk
55 g/2 oz butter, melted
1 bunch spring onions, chopped
ground black pepper

>1 Preheat the oven to 190°C/375°F/ Gas Mark 5. Grease a 23-cm/9-inch square baking tin.

>2 Sift the cornmeal, flour, baking powder, celery salt and pepper into a bowl and stir in 40 g/1½ oz of the Parmesan.

>3 Beat together the eggs, milk and melted butter.

>4 Add the egg mixture to the dry ingredients and stir well to mix evenly.

>5 Stir in the chopped spring onions and spread the mixture evenly into the tin.

>6 Sprinkle the remaining Parmesan over the mixture. Bake in the preheated oven for 30–35 minutes, or until firm and golden. Cut the cornbread into squares and serve warm.

feta & olive scones

makes 8 scones

ingredients

400 g/14 oz self-raising flour
¼ tsp salt
85 g/3 oz butter, plus extra for
  greasing

40 g/1½ oz pitted black olives,
  chopped
40 g/1½ oz sun-dried tomatoes in
  oil, drained and chopped

85 g/3 oz feta cheese
  (drained weight), crumbled
200 ml/7 fl oz milk, plus extra
  for glazing

>1 Preheat the oven to 220°C/425°F/ Gas Mark 7. Grease a baking sheet.

>2 Sift the flour and salt into a bowl. Add the butter and rub together until the mixture resembles breadcrumbs.

>3 Stir in the olives, tomatoes and feta. Add the milk, a little at a time, and mix to form a soft dough.

>4 Roll out on a floured surface to a 3-cm/1¼-inch thick rectangle. Cut into 6-cm/2½-inch squares. Place on the prepared baking sheet, brush with milk and bake for 12–15 minutes, until golden. Serve the scones while still warm.

stromboli with salami, roasted peppers & cheese

makes 1 loaf

ingredients

500 g/1 lb 2 oz strong white flour, sifted

6 g sachet fast-action dried yeast

2 tsp sea salt flakes

3 tbsp olive oil, plus extra for brushing

350 ml/12 fl oz lukewarm water

filling

85 g/3 oz thinly sliced Italian salami

175 g/6 oz mozzarella cheese, chopped

25 g/1 oz basil leaves

2 red peppers, roasted, peeled, deseeded and sliced

freshly ground black pepper

>1 Grease a bowl and a baking sheet. Place the flour, yeast and 1½ teaspoons of the salt in a bowl. Add the oil and water, a little at a time, and mix to form a soft dough.

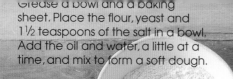

>2 Turn out the dough onto a lightly floured surface and knead for 10 minutes, until smooth and elastic. Shape the dough into a ball, place in the greased bowl, cover and leave in a warm place for 1 hour, or until doubled in volume.

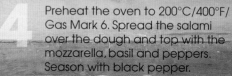

>3 Turn out the dough onto a lightly floured surface, knockback and knead for 2–3 minutes. Cover and leave for 10 minutes. Roll out the dough to a rectangle measuring 38 x 25 cm/15 x 10 inches in size, 1 cm/½ inch thick.

>4 Preheat the oven to 200°C/400°F/ Gas Mark 6. Spread the salami over the dough and top with the mozzarella, basil and peppers. Season with black pepper.

>5 Roll the dough up firmly from the long side, pinch the ends and place on the prepared baking sheet with the join underneath. Cover and leave for 10 minutes. Pierce the roll deeply several times with a skewer.

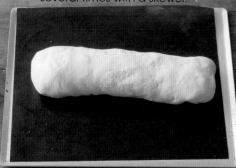

>6 Brush with oil and sprinkle with the remaining salt. Bake in the preheated oven for 30–35 minutes, or until firm and golden. Transfer to a wire rack to cool. Serve while still warm, cut into thick slices.

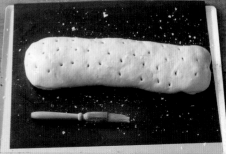

chocolate & saffron brioches

makes 12 brioches

ingredients

pinch of saffron strands

3 tbsp boiling water

250 g/9 oz strong plain flour

pinch of salt

1 tbsp caster sugar

6 g sachet easy-blend dried yeast

2 eggs, beaten

55 g/2 oz butter, melted

6 squares plain dark chocolate, halved (30 g/1 oz total)

milk, for glazing

>1 Add the saffron to the boiling water and leave to cool completely. Grease twelve holes of a bun tray and a bowl.

>2 Sift the flour, salt and sugar into a bowl and stir in the yeast. Add the saffron, saffron liquid, eggs and remaining butter and mix to form a soft dough.

>3 Knead until smooth, place in the greased bowl, cover and leave for 1–1½ hours, or until doubled in volume.

>4 Knead briefly then shape three quarters of the dough into twelve balls. Place into the bun tray and press a piece of chocolate into the centre of each.

>5 Shape the remaining dough into twelve smaller balls. Brush with milk and press on top of the dough in the tray, sealing well.

>6 Cover with clingfilm and leave for 1½ hours, or until doubled in volume. Meanwhile, preheat the oven to 200°C/400°F/Gas Mark 6. Brush the brioches with milk and bake in the preheated oven for 12–15 minutes, until golden brown. Serve warm.

scones

makes 9 scones

ingredients

450 g/1 lb plain flour, plus extra for
dusting
½ tsp salt
2 tsp baking powder

55 g/2 oz butter
2 tbsp caster sugar
250 ml/9 fl oz milk, plus extra
for glazing

strawberry jam and clotted cream,
to serve

>1 Preheat the oven to 220°C/425°F/ Gas Mark 7. Sift the flour, salt and baking powder into a bowl. Add the butter and rub together until the mixture resembles breadcrumbs.

>2 Stir in the sugar. Add the milk and mix to form a soft dough.

>3 Turn out the dough onto a floured surface and very lightly flatten it until it is 1 cm/½ inch thick. Cut out scones using a 6-cm/2½-inch biscuit cutter and place on a lined baking sheet.

>4 Brush with a little milk and bake in the preheated oven for 10–12 minutes, until well risen and golden brown. Leave to cool on a wire rack. Serve warm with strawberry jam and clotted cream.

crown loaf

serves 9

ingredients

2 tbsp butter, diced, plus extra
   for greasing
225 g/8 oz strong white flour
½ tsp salt
7 g/¼ oz easy-blend dried yeast

125 ml/4 fl oz lukewarm milk
1 egg, lightly beaten
115 g/4 oz icing sugar
1–2 tbsp lemon juice

filling

4 tbsp butter, softened
50 g/1¾ oz soft light brown sugar
2 tbsp chopped hazelnuts
1 tbsp crystallized ginger
50 g/1¾ oz chopped mixed peel
1 tbsp dark rum or brandy

>1 Grease a bowl and a baking sheet. Sift the flour and salt into a bowl. Stir in the yeast. Add the butter and rub together until the mixture resembles breadcrumbs. Add the milk and egg and mix to form a dough. Form the dough into a ball.

>2 Place the dough in the greased bowl, cover and leave in a warm place for 40 minutes, or until doubled in volume. Knead lightly for 1 minute, then roll out the dough to a rectangle measuring 30 x 23 cm/ 12 x 9 cm.

>3 For the filling, beat the butter and sugar together until light and fluffy. Stir in the hazelnuts, ginger, mixed peel and rum. Spread the filling over the dough, leaving a 2.5-cm/ 1-inch border.

>4 Roll up the dough, starting from one of the long edges, into a sausage shape. Cut into slices at 5-cm/2-inch intervals and place in a circle on the prepared baking tray with the slices just touching.

>5 Cover and leave in a warm place for 30 minutes. Meanwhile, preheat the oven to 190°C/375°F/Gas Mark 5. Bake the loaf in the preheated oven for 20–30 minutes, or until golden.

>6 For the icing, mix the sugar with enough lemon juice to form a thin icing. Leave the loaf to cool slightly before drizzling with the icing. Allow the icing to set before serving.

cherry & peel spirals

makes 8 spirals

ingredients

100 g/3½ oz glacé cherries,
  chopped
40 g/1½ oz chopped mixed peel
55 g/2 oz soft light brown sugar
finely grated rind of 1 lemon

1 tsp ground allspice
250 g/9 oz strong plain flour
½ tsp salt
6 g sachet easy-blend dried yeast

125 ml/4 fl oz lukewarm milk, plus
  extra for brushing
1 egg, beaten
3 tbsp melted butter,
  plus extra for greasing

>1 ... bowl. Mix together the cherries, peel, sugar, lemon rind and allspice.

>2 ...in the flour and salt into a bowl. Stir in the yeast. Add the milk, egg and 2 tablespoons of the butter and mix to form a soft dough.

>3 Turn out the dough onto a lightly floured surface and knead for 10 minutes, until smooth and elastic. Shape the dough into a ball, place in the greased bowl, cover and leave in a warm place for 1–1½ hours, or until doubled in volume.

>4 Knead lightly for 1 minute, then roll out the dough to a rectangle measuring 25 x 30 cm/10 x 12 inches. Brush with the remaining butter and sprinkle with the fruit mixture.

>5 Roll up from the long side. Cut into eight slices and arrange in the tin. Cover and leave to rise in a warm place until doubled in volume. Preheat the oven to 190°C/375°F/Gas Mark 5.

>6 Brush with milk and bake in the preheated oven for 25–30 minutes, until firm and golden. Transfer to a wire rack to cool. Gently pull the buns apart and serve.

cinnamon spiced orange beignets

makes 8 beignets

ingredients

250 g/9 oz plain flour
1 tsp easy-blend dried yeast
1½ tbsp caster sugar
125 ml/4 fl oz lukewarm milk

1 egg, beaten
finely grated rind of 1 small orange
1 tsp orange flower water
40 g/1½ oz butter, melted

sunflower oil, for deep frying
cinnamon sugar, for sprinkling
orange slices or segments,
   to serve

>1. Sift the flour into a bowl and stir in the yeast and sugar.

>2. Add the milk, egg, orange rind, flower water and butter, and mix to a soft dough, kneading until smooth.

>3. Cover and leave in a warm place until doubled in volume. Roll out on a lightly floured surface to 1 cm/½ inch in thickness, and cut into eight 7.5-cm/3-inch squares.

>4. Heat the oil to 180°C/350°F. Fry the beignets in batches until golden brown. Remove with a slotted spoon and drain on kitchen paper. Sprinkle with cinnamon sugar and serve hot with orange slices or segments.

Index